Original Hendrix

Steve Tarshis.

GW00482006

Wise Publications.
London, New York, Sydney,
Cologne.

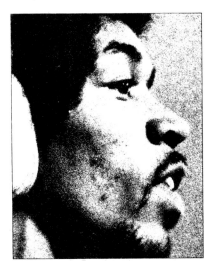

Foreword
Page 4

To the spirit of Jimi Hendrix;
and to those who raise their freak flag high.

This book © copyright 1982 by Wise
Publications.
Text © copyright 1982 by Steve Tarshis.

Exclusive distributors:
Music Sales Limited,
8/9 Frith Street, London W1V 5TZ,
England.
Music Sales Corporation,
24 East 22nd Street, New York,
N.Y. 10010, USA.
Music Sales Pty. Limited,
27 Clarendon Street, Artarmon,
2064, Australia.

ISBN 0-7119-0015-9.
UK Order No. AM 30040.

All rights reserved. No part of this
book may be reproduced in any form
or by any electronic or mechanical
means, including information
storage and retrieval systems,
without permission in writing from
the publisher, except by a reviewer
who may quote brief passages in a
review.
Printed in Great Britain by
Thetford Press Limited,
Thetford, Norfolk.

Bends and Vibrato

Error

Error

Bends and Vibrato

Error

Bends and Vibrato
Page 31

Low-Note Riffs
Page 45

Error

ErrorPage 50

Hendrix and the Blues

"Little Wing" A Hendrix Classic
Page 55

Page 61

The Recordings of Jimi Hendrix

Error

Error

Error3

Error3

IN SEATTLE, 1957/JAMES ALLEN HENDRIX

Foreword

This book focuses on Jimi Hendrix as a *guitarist.* Its main purpose is to act as a guide for the guitar player who seeks to expand his own resources by exploring the techniques of the greatest and most innovative of all electric guitarists: Jimi Hendrix.

Hendrix more than anyone else has defined what today's rock guitar is about. He was the first to explore fully the use of feedback and distortion, as well as the use of such devices as the wah-wah pedal. But just as importantly, Hendrix was a great musician who utilized these effects as means to his artistic ends, not as ends in themselves. This was ever-present in my mind while writing, and I hope that the reader will also keep it in mind.

All notations are made in guitar tablature and standard notation, and both systems may be utilized in working out the examples and transcriptions.

This book was truly a labor of love and I hope that you will be as inspired reading it as I was writing it. Examining Jimi's style will benefit all guitarists, no matter what their style, because Jimi the Innovator was also Jimi the Keeper of the Flame. Hendrix brought with him a whole tradition of blues, gospel, and R&B styles with which he was totally familiar. This tradition was always evident in his work and any musician will enrich his own vocabulary by tapping this resource too.

Jimi Hendrix: An American Artist

James Marshall Hendrix was born in Seattle, Washington on November 27, 1942. A black man who was to become a rock and roll hero, a flashy superstar who seemed to be *the* essence of the spaced-out, druggy sixties, Hendrix was, in reality, quiet, withdrawn, and somewhat inarticulate, except when he had a guitar in his hands. Then he was transformed into a musician of the highest order, an artist who could hear something different, something new that no one else had yet imagined. He became a poet whose song lyrics were like a new-age Coleridge—a bluesman from some dark place, who had been magically transported to a land of fairy tale images of color and sound. Jimi Hendrix brought these images to life by combining a venerable black tradition of rhythm, funk, and showmanship with the rising white youth culture of imagery, technology, and the pursuit of freedom. But Hendrix seemed to be the unwilling visionary, a space-age witchdoctor caught in the flux of several converging cultures. For a moment in time, he caught the imagination of millions with whispered phrases and raging metal sears of unheard-of musical sound that was always the blues, even if some of his unsuspecting listeners didn't know it. For many were swayed by image alone, the incredible, sensual, sexual power. Jimi Hendrix was everything an American mother could have nightmares about.

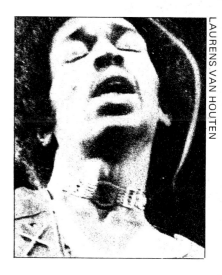

LAURENS VAN HOUTEN

LAURENS VAN HOUTEN

When Jimi Hendrix became ultimately, and inevitably, the victim of media overkill and future-shock disease, when he finally fell prey to the image he portrayed, he left us something beyond the flash. Through his music, he showed us how guitar would now be played in the new future by creating a whole new palette of musical styles and directions. He was the newest link in the guitar chain which included Django Reinhardt, Charlie Christian, and Wes Montgomery. He was part of the lineage of American music genius-innovators—Armstrong, Ellington, Parker, Miles, Trane: black men in America. Only America, where weird combinations of cultural events come together to produce the world's music, could have made the blues; and only America could have produced Jimi Hendrix.

Jimi's dad, a landscape gardener, had a large collection of blues and R&B records. Both his mother, who died when he was young, and his aunt played piano at the local Baptist church. When his father discovered the twelve-year-old Hendrix playing a broomstick, he promptly traded in his own saxophone and bought the boy his first acoustic guitar. James Marshall began to play. He ended up playing left-handed (strumming with the left hand, fingering with the right), playing in several local rock groups around Seattle and in British Columbia. Nobody remembers him as being that great. When Jimi dropped out of school and enlisted in the Air Force at seventeen, he didn't even take his guitar, although soon enough he wrote his father asking for the instrument, saying he was going crazy without it.

In the service, Hendrix continued his practice of jamming with anyone and everyone, something he religiously pursued even after he became a rock celebrity. Jimi was a paratrooper, but after little more than two years with Uncle Sam, he hurt his back and foot in a jump and was discharged early. Once he was out of the service, Hendrix began to play the "chitlin" circuit with assorted R&B acts, ending up in New York with King Curtis, majesty of the saxophone. By the time he was twenty-five, Jimi had played with Ike and Tina Turner, Little Richard, Joey Dee, Jackie Wilson, James Brown, Wilson Pickett, B.B. King, and Curtis Knight.

WITH CURTIS KNIGHT & THE SQUIRES

But something must have been raging inside the soul of this black kid who was remembered by his fellow backup musicians as being shy and unassuming. "I got tired of feeding back 'In the Midnight Hour'," he told an interviewer later.

In 1966 he began to play with his own group. "Jimmy James and the Blue Flames" played around the Village in places like the Cafe Wha?. Veteran musicians in the area still tell stories about this quiet fellow who always dragged around his guitar and would play up on his fire escape all through the hot summer city nights.

Meanwhile in the clubs, Jimmy James's wild posturing, experiments in volume, and phenomenal blues ability, were beginning to have an effect. He even sang now, something he was always self-conscious about until he heard Bob Dylan. Then he figured that if Dylan could sing in that weird kind of voice, why couldn't he? People began to talk. One night "Chas" Chandler, the bass player with the Animals, came in. He told Hendrix he wanted to take him to England and make him a star. He would get him a passport, an airplane ticket, some money, and besides, Chas would introduce him to Eric Clapton. So it was agreed, and Chandler was as good as his word.

Jimmy James became Jimi Hendrix.

Chandler got two English boys to play in Jimi's group. Noel Redding was a guitarist who, until then, had never played bass. Mitch Mitchell was chosen as the drummer, an explosive, wildly imaginative player who sounded something like a rock Elvin Jones. The Experience was born. Four days later they opened at the Olympia, then the biggest club on the Continent. The Experience played "Midnight Hour," "Land of 1000 Dances," "Everyone Needs Someone to Love," and "Respect"—songs right out of the "chitlin" circuit, but played like no one else had performed them before or since. "Hey Joe" and "Purple Haze" were released as singles and became hits. The Experience toured Europe, breaking attendance records everywhere. In Europe, Jimi Hendrix was literally an overnight sensation. Ironically (but typically) he was still virtually unknown in the land of his birth.

That situation was rectified soon enough.

Lou Adler, one of the coproducers of the Monterey Pop Festival, had heard from Paul McCartney about "some guy in England playing guitar with his teeth." He booked the Experience for their American debut. Jimi performed on the last night of the festival and his set has been recorded and released on an album that also included Otis Redding's show. Pete Johnson, of Warner Brothers, wrote in the liner notes:

> "Jimi Hendrix, Mitch Mitchell, and Noel Redding were the rage of England in that summer of love and psychedelia but they had yet to play the United States and thus were no more than a rumor to most of the Monterey crowd. Their appearance at the festival was magical: the way they looked, the way they performed and the way they sounded were light years away from anything anyone had seen before. The Jimi Hendrix Experience owned the future and the audience knew it in an instant. The banks of amplifiers and speakers wailing and groaning as Hendrix's fingers scurried across the strings of his guitar gave the trio's music as much density as other rock groups were getting out of studio eight-track tape machines. And of course, Hendrix is a masterful, though seemingly off-hand performer. Pete Townsend [sic] of the Who had become famous for destroying his guitar. Hendrix carried the ritual a couple of fantasies farther with lighter fluid and dramatic playing positions in "Wild Thing." When Jimi left the stage, he had graduated from rumor to legend."

Jimi had set his guitar and the American public's imagination on fire.

In a beautiful display of music business naiveté, Jimi was put on tour with none other than the Monkees. This was, of course, disastrous, although it's interesting to speculate on what effect Jimi Hendrix had on the developing

WITH NOEL REDDING/PETER STUART

KATHY ETCHINGHAM, JIMI'S FIRST ENGLISH GIRLFRIEND

WITH MICK JAGGER/ALEC BYRNE

BARRIE WENTZELL

H. GOODWIN

LAURENS VAN HOUTEN

psyches of thousands of young Monkees fans. The Experience were pulled out of the tour, (some sort of story involving the Daughters of the American Revolution was fabricated) to play to packed houses on their own. "Purple Haze" and the album from which it came, the immortal *Are You Experienced*, both became hits in America.

Jimi was now a genuine rock superstar, playing to enthusiastic crowds both in the States and in Europe. The ubiquitous Youth Culture was totally captivated by his outrageous costumes, his incredible stage theatrics, and his totally unique musical conception. The three recordings he made on Warner

Reprise during this period stand forever, not only because of the guitar work, which was revolutionary in itself, but as total musical entities. Hendrix, more than any other rock performer before or since, utilized the developing technology of the studio and of the electronic guitar, to make his vision come across as larger than life. Yet, the earthiness of the bluesman and the poetry of the mystic visionary were always at the fore. Hendrix ultimately makes his mark as an artist who had total command over his tools. Hendrix was *Rolling Stone*'s Performer of the Year in 1968, a distinction he had already won in Europe's *Disc* and *Melody Maker* magazines. *Are You Experienced*, *Axis: Bold as Love*, and *Electric Ladyland* LP's all went gold.

Yet, as the pace of Hendrix's journey became more harried, the duality that had always been characteristic of Jimi began to show itself more and more. As with any artist, Jimi's vision was going far beyond what his vast audience (not to mention his slew of managers, agents, etc.) had come to expect of him. His image was really beginning to plague him.

Always willing to hang out and jam with all kinds of musicians, Jimi began to express desires to make new kinds of music. The summer and fall of '69 were spent in relative seclusion in upstate New York with a community of musicians assembled by Hendrix. Jazz avant-gardists, blues rootsmen, and all manner of eclectics were harbored together to make a new kind of "sky church music." "I don't want to be a clown anymore," said Jimi, "I don't want to be a rock and roll star." Somehow, though, the community approach didn't quite work out.

In late 1969, the Experience was officially disbanded. Along with Buddy Miles on drums and Billy Cox, an old service buddy, on bass, the Band of Gypsies was formed. Their performance at the Fillmore, preserved on the *Band of Gypsies* LP, was hailed by promoter Bill Graham as the best he had ever witnessed in his hall. Jimi was somewhat less enthusiastic, though; the group never toured and Hendrix seemed continually unsure of what direction to take. A low point was reached when Hendrix walked off stage during a Band of Gypsies performance at the Moratorium concert at Madison Square Garden. "We're just not getting it together," he told the crowd.

H. GOODWIN

The reforming of the Experience was hyped for a time, but this didn't materialize either. In the spring and summer of '70 Hendrix toured with Mitch Mitchell and Billy Cox, playing the Isle of Wight festival in England in August. Then, on September 18, 1970 Jimi Hendrix was pronounced dead upon arrival at St. Mary Abbots Hospital, Kensington, England. The cause of death was "inhalation of vomit due to barbiturate intoxication." Some say that his death could have been prevented, that he was alive in the ambulance on the way to the hospital but he was put in a position that made breathing impossible.

It's easy for many to view Jimi's death as a suicide caused by despair and frustration. From all evidence, however, this was not the case. Jimi had not taken anywhere near enough of the barbiturates to kill him. Apparently, he just didn't wake up in enough time to prevent his own drowning. More important, all indications are that Hendrix was at this time on the verge of a whole new approach to his art and his career. He was even in the process of clearing up his muddled business affairs.

WITH KATHY ETCHINGHAM

Although there have been other albums since his death (mostly pastiches from the mountains of tapes made during his career), Jimi's last fully realized release, *Cry of Love*, is one of his best and most unusual — full of the promise of further development had Hendrix been able to continue his artistic growth.

AT ALBERT HALL, LONDON/ERIC HAYES

Hendrix the Guitarist

Contrary to what you might expect, Jimi did not rely on gadgetry to achieve his unique sound. Witnesses report that Hendrix was able to create his vast array of sounds with a Fender Stratocaster, a Fuzz Face distortion unit, a Cry Baby wah-wah pedal, and a Univibe pedal. In clubs and jams, Jimi used smaller amplifiers like the Twin Reverb. For concerts, stacks of Marshall amps with everything turned up were used. Jimi almost always used a Strat for live performance and studio work, but occasionally he played a Gibson Flying V. He was especially adept at using the tremolo bar on the Strat to get some of the space-bends that characterized some of his work. It seems also that the guitar was tuned down a half step, perhaps to bend notes more easily, but more likely because Jimi preferred this kind of sound.

Jimi is often exclusively associated with distortion and feedback effects and, although this was only a part of the Hendrix sound, at the time it seemed completely revolutionary. In fact, Hendrix was a pioneer of volume playing and electronic effects, and his work in these areas almost single-handedly created the rock guitar idiom.

Live, Jimi was sometimes an uneven performer, and some say that his best playing was done in after-hours jams with everyone from John McLaughlin to Johnny Winter to Roland Kirk. You can hear examples of his live playing on *Band of Gypsies*, on the Monterey album, and on the Woodstock LP, which includes the amazing Hendrix rendition of the "Star Spangled Banner," complete with bombs bursting and rockets taking off. I'd also recommend the "Voodoo Child" performance on *Electric Ladyland.* This blues-rooted piece was improvised live in a studio with a film crew also present.

Hendrix Chords

Jimi Hendrix was a master musician who could make his guitar sound like a full band, often playing rhythm, lead and bass parts at the same time. Hendrix, of course, wrote most of his own songs and they were very much an outgrowth of his guitar style. Hendrix developed certain ways of playing chords that fit his style and helped produce his unique sound. Often these chords were derived from other styles (such as R&B) with which Hendrix had been involved during his earlier days as a backup musician. Some of these chords came from jazz, and some he just made up. No doubt Hendrix's unique chord thinking came from the unusual way that he held the guitar: upside down and backwards!

The Sharp Ninth

One of Jimi's favorite chords is the *sharp ninth chord*. This is the main chord you hear in such songs as "Purple Haze" and "Foxey Lady." This chord is much used by jazz players and such R&B masters as James Brown. The sharp ninth chord is an extension of a dominant seventh chord (such as C7, D7, A7, etc.). Another note, the sharp ninth, is added above the dominant seventh. This note is an octave plus a minor third from the root of the chord. Therefore, to form an E7#9 chord we add the note G above an E7 chord.

Here are some examples of sharp ninth chords.

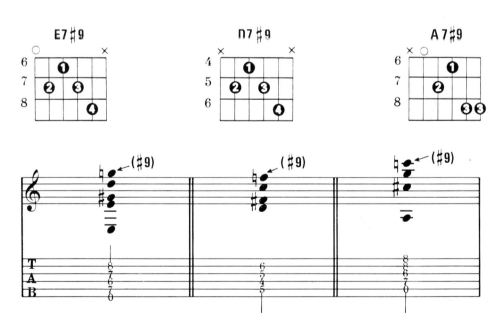

BARRIE WENTZELL

The sharp ninth produces a sharp, angry, metallic funk sound that Hendrix used often. The following example is a riff similar to the one used in "Purple Haze." It is based on an E7#9 chord. Notice that the chord is combined with a lick on the lower strings that a bass player would play. This is typical of the way that Jimi constructs his songs. The low-note bass lick may be doubled by the bass player to produce a full sound like that of the Experience. An accent mark (>) over a chord means to strike the notes forcefully with your pick. If you are using an electric guitar and you have a distortion device (either a pedal or one built into an amplifier), use it when you play this example to get the most Hendrix-like sound.

Don't forget to follow the repeat signs (‖: :‖). They indicate that the section is to be repeated.

Open Strings

Another Hendrix chord device makes use of open strings. The next example shows a G chord that contains the open third string. This chord has no third. The note B, the third of a G Major chord, is purposely left out. The absence of the third produces a sound that is neither major nor minor.

In the following example the G voicing with the open string is moved down two frets to produce an F chord. This F chord again has no third and the open G string is retained, producing the drone effect that Hendrix used so often. You can hear this effect in "Love or Confusion" on *Are You Experienced.*

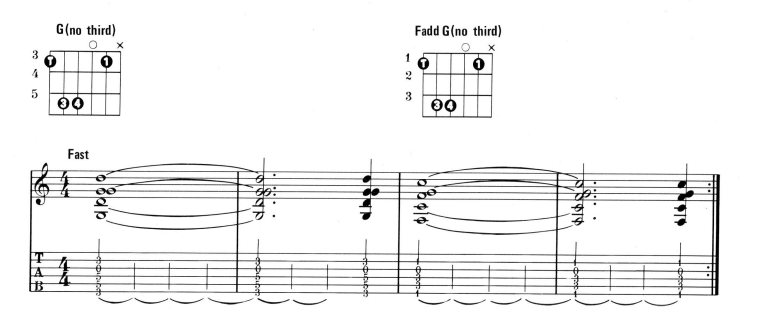

Chords Without Thirds

Another Hendrix trademark is chords with no thirds, with or without open strings. Here we have a voicing without thirds combined with a traditional major-chord voicing in the intro to the Hendrix classic "The Wind Cries Mary."

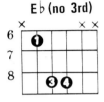

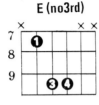

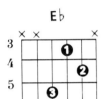

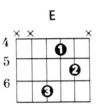

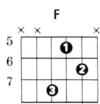

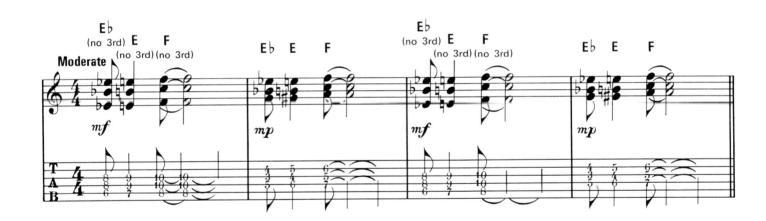

The Major Ninth

We've seen how Hendrix could change a chord and make it his own by subtracting a note. He could also juice up a chord by adding a note. Adding a ninth (an octave plus a whole step) to a major triad produces a *major ninth chord*, a sound that Hendrix used often. To a C Major chord add the note D to get a major ninth chord (also seen as "C add nine"). You can hear Hendrix use this chord at the beginning of "Third Stone from the Sun." The next example uses the major ninth chord sound. As in "Third Stone from the Sun," major ninths are very effective when the bass and drums play at a fast, jazzy tempo and the ninths are held out as whole notes. (In each of the following chords the pinky holds down the ninth.)

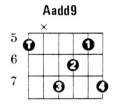

Aadd9

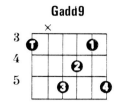

Gadd9

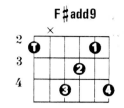

F#add9

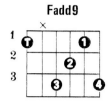

Fadd9

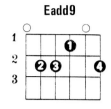

Eadd9

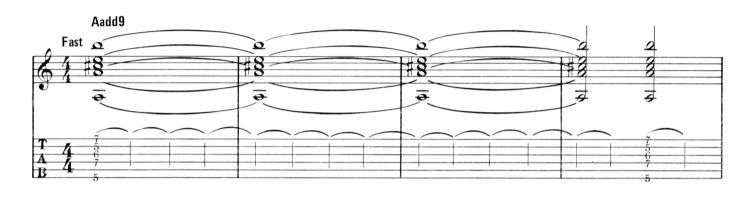

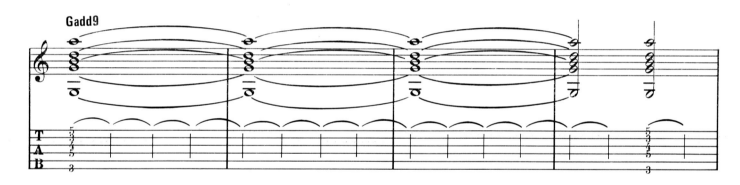

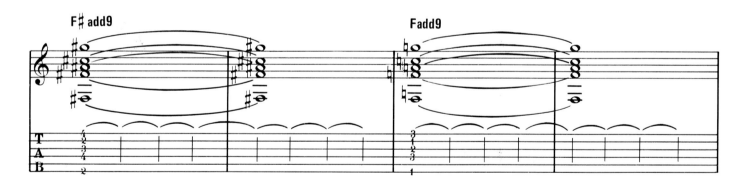

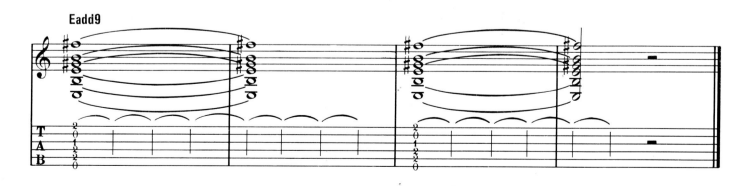

Hendrix gets another sound from the major ninth chord by subtracting the third, as in the next example. Jimi creates an "eastern" sound by sliding from one chord to another. To play a *slide* (SL) pick the first chord notated (the one with the accent mark over it) and move the hand up or down to the next chord shown, without picking again. Two chords are played, but only one is picked. You can hear this effect in the intro to "Castles Made of Sand."

The "add nine, no third" is fingered as shown below. The third string must be muted (not sounded). This is accomplished by pressing the tip of the first finger (which is playing the note on the second string) against the third string and preventing it from being sounded when the pick strums the rest of the chord.

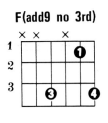

F(add9 no 3rd)

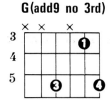

G(add9 no 3rd)

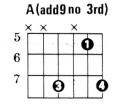

A(add9 no 3rd)

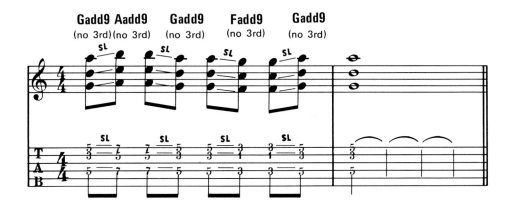

Gadd9 Aadd9 Gadd9 Fadd9 Gadd9
(no 3rd)(no 3rd) (no 3rd) (no 3rd) (no 3rd)

BARRIE WENTZELL

20

Hammer-Ons and Pull-Offs

Jimi Hendrix achieved an amazingly full sound from his guitar. Besides playing unusual voicings and chords, he could make the most of ordinary chords and really bring them alive. His embellishment techniques are very applicable to all kinds of playing styles and situations, as many are derived from early R&B masters whose influence on Hendrix was immense.

Let's start with a typical major-chord formation. This is an F chord. What we're interested in is that the fingering is movable; that is, by moving it up and down the neck we get different chord names — F# at the sixth fret, E♭ at the third fret, etc.

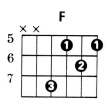

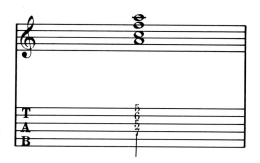

Working with this basic fingering, we're going to use some hammer-ons to get some new sounds. A *hammer-on* (H) is played by picking a note, then immediately fingering another note on the same string and making another sound, without picking again. In the example below, pick the note C on the fifth fret, third string (use your first finger) and then immediately finger the note D (third string, seventh fret) hard enough to produce a clean sound without picking a second time. Congratulations, you have just played a hammer-on! Practice until you can play it clean and hard.

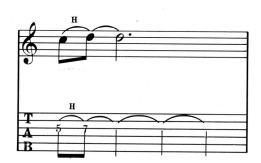

Our next objective is to play this hammer-on within the voicing of the F chord that we saw before. To do this, first strum the F chord, then strum the upper three strings of the voicing, hammering-on to the note D. Now, play the first three strings again in the usual way. Finally, add the lower note of the voicing (A on the seventh fret, D string) by playing another hammer-on. This last hammer-on is accomplished by fingering the note G (with the first finger that is also holding down the top three strings) and hammering-on to the A with the third finger. This whole process is illustrated overleaf.

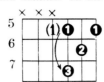

strum an F chord   **strum the upper three strings and hammer-on the D**   **play first three strings again**

Strum the second, third, and fourth strings, hammering-on to the lower note (A on the fourth string, seventh fret) as shown.

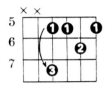

Let's look at this in notation.

This technique is used quite often by Jimi, especially in ballads. Listen to "The Wind Cries Mary" or "Little Wing" and you'll see what I mean. The next example is an exercise that will help you get this riff down in several positions.

F   **E♭**   **D♭**

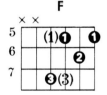   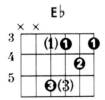   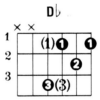

C

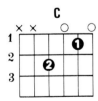

Slow

22

Hendrix uses this technique so often, and it is so applicable to all styles of music, that it's worth our while to apply the same chord embellishments to the other two major-chord fingerings.

The *pull-off* (P) is the reverse of the hammer-on. A note is picked, and the left-hand finger is immediately removed with enough pressure to sound the string again, producing a note that is a fret (or several frets) below the original note on the same string. In the example below, the D (third string, seventh fret) is picked and fingered with the third left-hand finger. It is then immediately removed and the C (third string, fifth fret) is sounded without picking again.

Now let's combine the hammer-on and the pull-off in a single-note run. This produces the modal sound that Hendrix uses often. (Listen to the solo in "Purple Haze".) In the example below, all the notes are played on the G string. The notes that have accents over them are the only ones that are picked with the right hand. The numbers refer to the left-hand fingering.

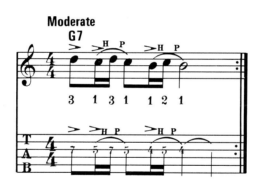

Combining the hammer-on and pull-off within a major-chord voicing is the kind of thing that enabled Hendrix to play rhythm and lead parts at the same time.

In the next example, notice that the first finger plays a small bar chord and the third finger plays the embellishments. First, a D Major voicing is strummed. Then, while still holding on to the chord with the first finger, a hammer-on/pull-off combination is executed with the third finger. Finally, another hammer-on is played on the fourth string, adding a note to the chord. The added note, B, makes this a D6 chord. The charts below illustrate the whole riff.

strum a D chord

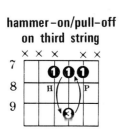

hammer–on/pull–off on third string

final hammer–on on the fourth string

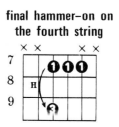

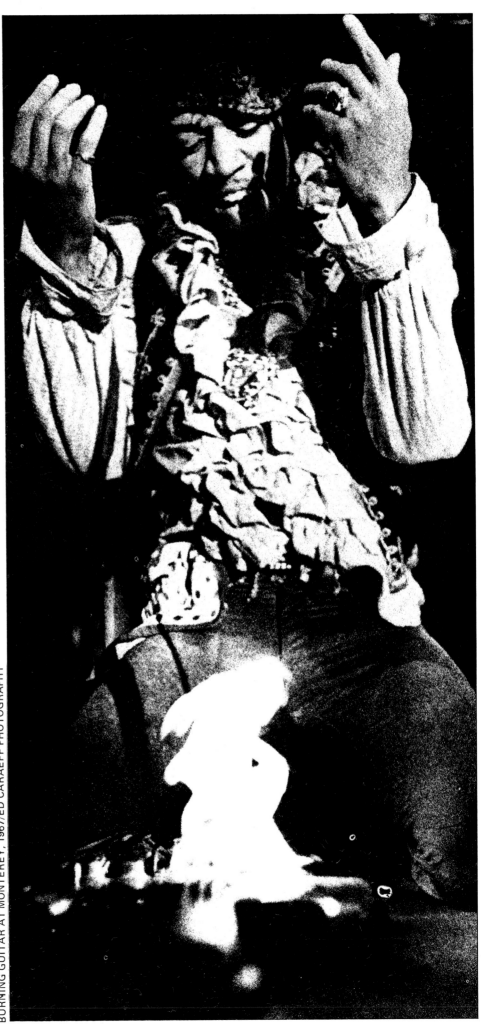

BURNING GUITAR AT MONTEREY, 1967/ED CARAEFF PHOTOGRAPHY

Notated and played in time,
the riff looks like this:

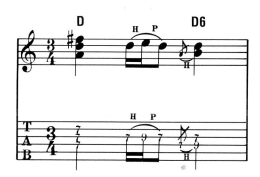

The example below will help you learn this riff.

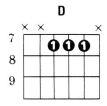
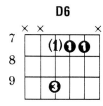
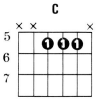

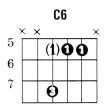
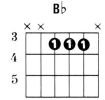
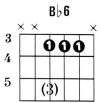

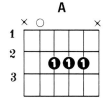

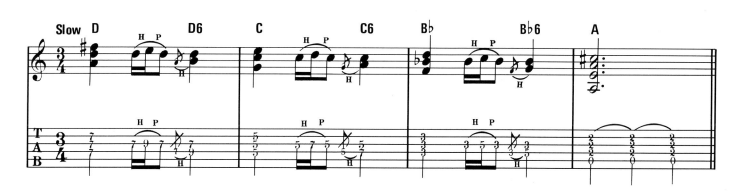

The next example shows how another major-chord fingering may be embellished Hendrix-style. In this case the pinky of the left hand plays a hammer-on/pull-off combination on the first string, and then plays an added sixth note on the second string. The basic chord is played as an *arpeggio*—that is, the notes of the chord are played one at a time instead of all at once. This helps get a really full sound out of a chord.

This next riff is illustrated in the charts below, using a basic C chord in eighth position (on the eighth fret).

finger this C chord through the entire riff

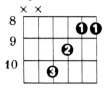

pick these two notes

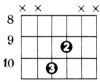

add this note while the previous notes ring through

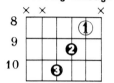

hammer-on/pull-off on the first string

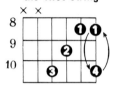

add this note on the second string

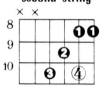

Notated and in time the lick looks like this:

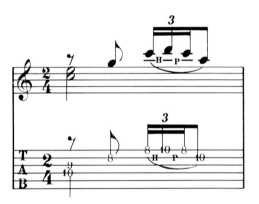

You can hear Hendrix play something like this next example during part of his masterful solo in "All Along the Watchtower."

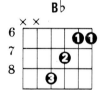

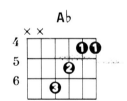

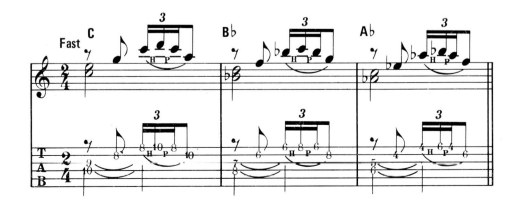

Symbols and Chord Charts

We're now ready to tackle "The Wind Cries Mary" which I've written out note for note from the intro right through the guitar solo. (After that the song pretty much repeats itself.) In this ballad Hendrix makes extended use of the chord embellishments that we've been talking about. I hope you own or can borrow a copy of *Are You Experienced*, Jimi's first major release and the record that most defines his style. The notation looks pretty complicated but is simplified by the repeated riffs and the similar positions that are used. The following chord and position charts will help you figure out the fingering to use. Arabic numbers refer to measures. Here are some of the other symbols:

Roman Numerals (I, II, III, etc.) = positions (fret numbers)

H = hammer-on

P = pull-off

SL = slide

B = bend.
There is one bend in the solo (an unusually small number for a Hendrix solo). To play a bend, finger the note that is in parentheses and bend it up until the sound of the following written note is heard. We will study Hendrix's bending technique in detail later on in the book.

〰 = vibrato.
This is a move that is essential to the Jimi Hendrix style. Vibrato is played by moving the indicated note up and down (in the direction of your head and toes). Hard pressure on the string is called for, so you'll have to develop strong finger muscles and practice hard to get a good vibrato. It's well worth it; just listen to Jimi's in measures 18, 20, 22, and 25. (More on vibrato later.)

These chord and fingering charts will help you work through the piece. Listen to the record! The first measures have been discussed previously so we'll start at the part marked [A] where the singing starts.

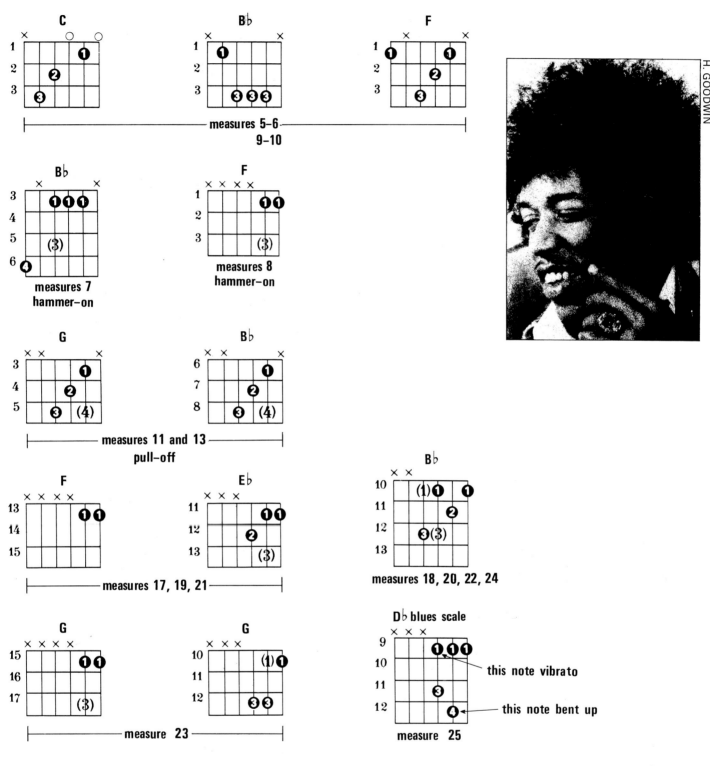

measures 5-6
9-10

measures 7
hammer-on

measures 8
hammer-on

measures 11 and 13
pull-off

measures 17, 19, 21

measures 18, 20, 22, 24

Db blues scale

this note vibrato

this note bent up

measure 25

This finger pattern shows up in much of Hendrix's single-note work, as we'll see later. It's a beautiful measure. Check out the bend and the vibrato!

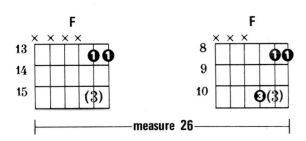

measure 26

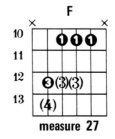

measure 27

"The Wind Cries Mary"
© Copyright 1967 Six Continents
Music Publishing Inc., USA.
For the UK, British Commonwealth
(excluding Canada & Australasia) & Eire
Interworld Music Limited,
15 Berkely Street, London W1.
All rights reserved.
International copyright secured.

H. GOODWIN

28

The Wind Cries Mary

Music by Jimi Hendrix

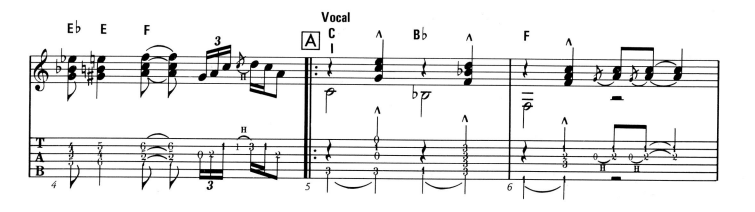

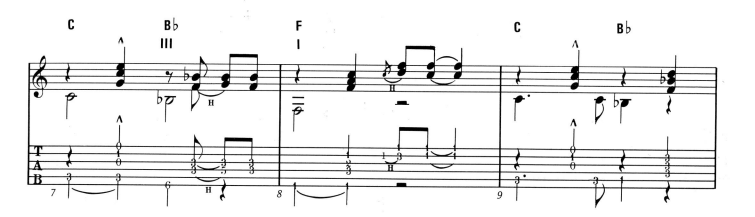

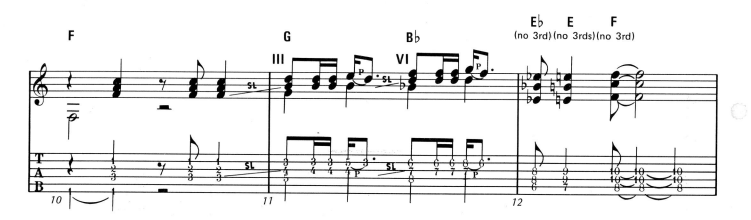

30

Bends and Vibrato

Jimi Hendrix has come to symbolize many of the effects that are now standard features in the vocabulary of rock and roll guitar playing. And, while some of these effects were derived from older blues and R&B styles, Jimi played them with such identifiable style and originality that he may as well have invented them, as far as succeeding generations of guitarists are concerned. Two of these effects are by far the most important: bends and vibrato.

In a Hendrix lead, hardly two notes in succession will go by without one or the other of these guitar staples. In fact, and this is an important key to the Hendrix sound: Bending and vibrato are often used simultaneously.

Vibrato

This sound is produced by vibrating the string with the left-hand finger after the note has already been struck with the pick. The direction of the finger movement is at a right angle to the neck (in line with the head and toes). This is different from the classical vibrato movement which is from side to side. Some players take the whole hand (except for the finger playing the note) off the neck to get the most leverage. Vibrato takes a lot of practice and must be carefully controlled. It can't be too fast, and the intonation (the "in-tuneness") must be right. If the vibrato is played with too much up and down movement it will sound sharp. Just listen to Jimi's. *Vibrato* is indicated by a lightning-bolt line (〰) over the note.

This next example contains a vibrato played with the first finger, a technique used often by Jimi to get a "stinging" sound. You can hear something like this lick in "Still Raining, Still Dreaming" where Hendrix uses the wah-

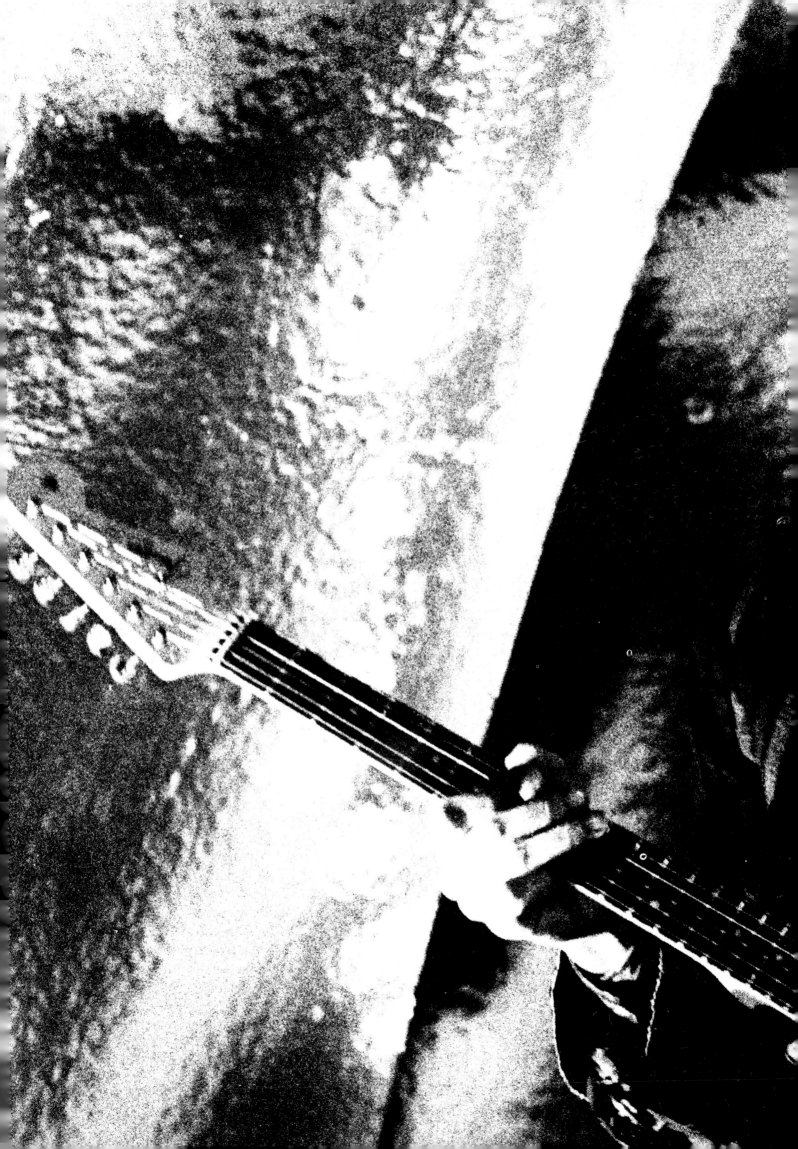

wah pedal and vibrato to create some great sounds. The notes come from
the blues scale in fifth position (key of A) as shown in the chart below.

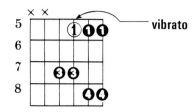

Moderate shuffle beat

Vibrato is often played with the third finger. This is an effective sound because, for one thing, the third finger is often the strongest. Strong fingers
are an important aspect of guitar control, and your muscles must be built up
by constant playing. (Jimi Hendrix had huge, long fingers.)

The next example features third-finger vibrato. You can hear something similar to it in "Voodoo Child (slight return)." This example uses D blues licks
played in third and fifth position as shown below.

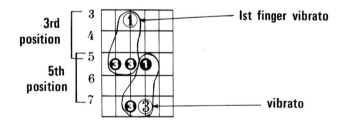

Bluesy

PHOTO OVERLEAF BY BARRIE WENTZELL

Hendrix utilizes an old blues lick to good effect in "Ain't No Telling." This lick features third-finger vibrato and a slide down to the low note. Play the example with a trebly, distorted tone. The fingering for this C blues line is in the chart below. These charts should be valuable clues for deciphering Hendrix's note choices and fingerings.

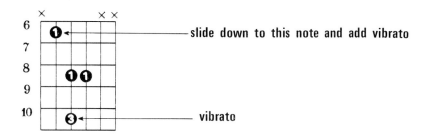

BARRIE WENTZELL

One of the best moments in "Foxey Lady" is when Jimi unleashes one of his mass distortion licks, as in the next example. It has a first-finger vibrato and a slide. (Notice how often Hendrix combines effects so that one heightens the sound of the other.) The lick is based on an E (#7#9) chord.

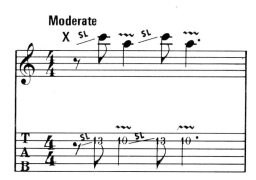

Bends

The effect that most typifies rock and roll guitar playing is the *bend,* and the master of bends was Jimi Hendrix. No other effect is as expressive, versatile, or as hard to master. It takes a lot of practice, listening, and finger strengthening, but once you get it down, you will realize that no matter how much time you put into it, the results were well worth it.

There are two main things you must think about when you are dealing with bending notes. The first is the physical effort involved in pushing the string up with your left hand finger. To help out here, you can experiment with light-gauge strings. To play Hendrix-type leads you will need a set of strings with a plain (not wound) G (third string). The first string, E, should be .08, .09, or .10. If you get a set with these properties you shouldn't have too much trouble bending the strings.

The second area of concern is pitch. The guitar is basically a fixed-pitch instrument. Because of the frets on the neck, when you finger a note you get a definite sound. (On instruments without frets, like the violin, you must find the exact space on the neck for each note, without the benefit of frets to guide you.) However, when you bend a note on the guitar, you are taking the note out of the convenient fret and bending it to change the pitch; and the pitch you arrive at depends on the amount of pressure you exert. To add to the problem, once you arrive at the correct pitch, you must hold the note there for a time. You must use your ear to know when you are bent up to the right note.

It sounds complicated, but with a little work you'll be able to develop your own approach. Of course, listening to Hendrix will help you get the right sound in your head, so it will start coming out of your guitar.

Let's begin with the third-finger bend, because the third finger is one of the strongest. Let's say that we are in eighth position on the neck, playing a C blues scale pattern, as in the chart below. The third-finger bend is circled as shown.

BARRIE WENTZELL

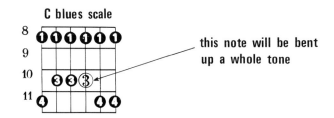

The note circled is F. A typical Hendrix move would be to bend this note up a whole step to G. This will be indicated as follows. The note to be fingered will be a small grace note or a note in parentheses. This note will be picked with the right hand and then immediately bent up (BU) to the larger note. In the example below, the F, fingered on the third string, tenth fret, is bent up to G.

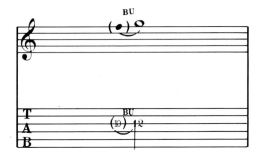

You can hear Jimi use this kind of bend in "Crosstown Traffic." He also sings the notes he plays to heighten the effect. Remember that the smaller written note is the one that is fingered, and the larger note is the one that you want to hear. Play through the lick slowly at first to get the idea. (Listen to the recording if you can.) The chords used are shown below.

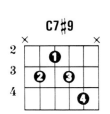 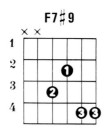 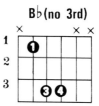

Crosstown Traffic (intro)
Music by Jimi Hendrix

This next bend is another that Jimi uses all the time. It's a little more difficult because it is played with the fourth finger (the pinky). This is the weakest finger for most people, but guitar players will want to build up all their left-hand fingers, especially the fourth. We'll try this one in the twelfth position inside an E blues fingering, one of Jimi's favorites. The chart below illustrates the fourth-finger bend. Remember that, as in the third-finger bend, these effects may be played all over the neck, not just in the position shown.

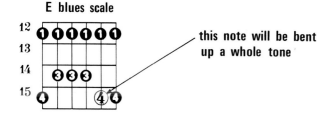

this note will be bent up a whole tone

"Crosstown Traffic"
© Copyright 1968 World Song
Publishing Inc., USA.
For the UK, British Commonwealth
(excluding Canada & Australasia) & Eire
Interworld Music Limited,
15 Berkely Street, London W1.
All rights reserved.
International copyright secured.

Like all bends, this is notated as shown below. The small note in parentheses is the one to be fingered (in this case, D on the second string, fifteenth fret). The note to be sounded is the larger one. Try to hear where the note is going *before* you play it.

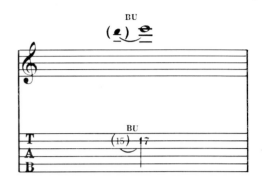

One of the secrets of Jimi's sound is that he *combined* bends and vibrato. The note is bent, and at the top of the bend the finger is moved up and down to produce vibrato.

Play the vibrato exactly as I described it previously, the only difference being that your left-hand finger is also playing a bend. When you bend a string, your left-hand finger will probably touch the string above on which no note is being played. Don't worry about that. When vibrato is added on top of the bend you will also be pushing up against another string. It will act as sort of a backstop, offering a little resistance but not affecting the sound. The main difficulty that you might have is strength and control. This is overcome by practice and ear training. Try to hear the effect you are going for, before you try to play it. The vibrato bend is notated as shown below. Be sure to put the vibrato on the note *after* you bend, while the string is still raised and the bent note is sounding.

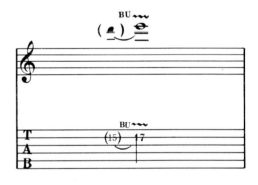

A good example of the fourth-finger bend with vibrato is heard in Jimi's solo in "Fire." In this lead there are also fourth-finger bends without vibrato, and first-finger vibrato with no bend. Again, notice how Hendrix carefully combines these effects. The whole solo may be played in the twelfth position.

Jimi Hendrix was a careful composer even in his wildest solos. Notice that various licks are repeated: The same vibrato bend begins every measure; the first two measures parallel the last two measures; the third and fourth, and fifth and sixth measures are basically the same. On the recording this break occurs after Jimi recites those famous lines, "Move over Rover, let Jimi take over. You know what I'm talking about, yeah, get on with it, Baby!" Many of his solo breaks are introduced in this manner, as the Hendrix guitar proceeds to graphically illustrate what Jimi has been singing about. The solo is played over a bass line that outlines an E7 chord.

"Fire"
© Copyright 1967 Six Continents
Music Publishing Inc., USA.
For the UK, British Commonwealth
(excluding Canada & Australasia) & Eire
Interworld Music Limited,
15 Berkely Street, London W1.
All rights reserved.
International copyright secured.

Fire (solo)

Music by Jimi Hendrix

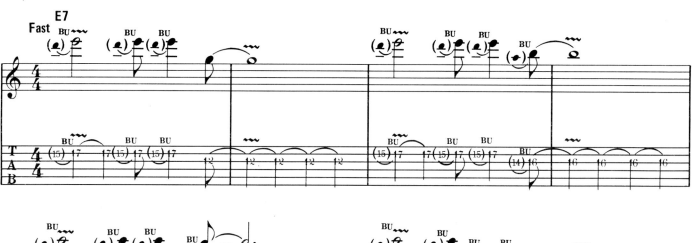

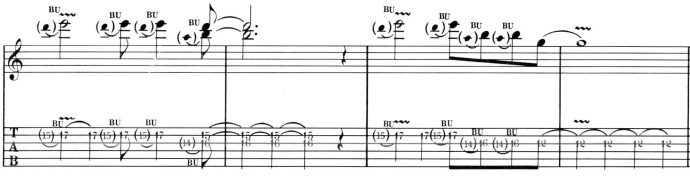

Double-Note Bends

A *double-note bend* is when one of the notes of a two-note chord is bent while the other note is held in place. We've just seen this effect at the end of the fifth measure in the "Fire" solo. The A is fingered on the third string, fourteenth fret, and the D is fingered on the second string, fifteenth fret. Both notes are picked with the right hand, and the A is immediately bent up to a B. If you play this you will recognize it as a sound that is used often in rock guitar and is well utilized by Hendrix to achieve a raw, funky attack. The diagram below illustrates how to play this lick.

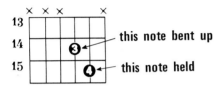

Notated, the lick looks like this:

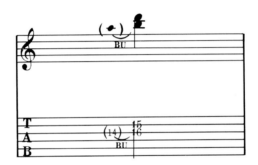

You can experiment with different ways to use the double-note bend. You might try using vibrato on the note that is bent to get some Hendrix-like sounds. Don't forget to try out different keys and positions on this and all other licks. It's one of the best ways that you can get to know the whole neck of the guitar.

You can hear Hendrix play something like the next example in "Night Bird Flying" from the *Cry of Love* album. Notice that the lick is played several times and then it is played as an arpeggio. Check the way the B♭ on the last beat of each measure is picked when it is already bent up (from the thirteenth fret) and then sounded as the third finger comes back to normal position. This is a bend down (BD). The lick is played in eleventh position against an E♭ chord. The fingering is given in the diagram below, and then notated in the example that follows.

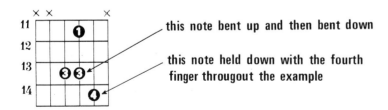

40

Octave Double Bends

The *octave double bend* is perhaps the most characteristic Hendrix sound. For any guitarist who is at all familiar with his work, it instantly conjures up the image of Jimi wailing. After Hendrix recordings became widely available, other rock guitarists immediately picked up on this sound (Carlos Santana, for example). It's a very powerful effect and has become a standard feature of the guitar vocabulary.

An octave double bend is played by fingering two notes that are a whole step apart on adjacent strings. Then, the note that is on the lower string is bent up until it is at the same pitch level as the note on the upper string. Often vibrato is added to the bent note.

Octave double bends are almost always played on either the first and second strings or on the second and third strings. In the example below, the octave double bend is played in the fifth position on the first and second strings. The first finger holds down A on the fifth fret, first string. The fourth finger playes the G on the second string, eighth fret, and then this note is bent up to A.

BARRIE WENTZELL

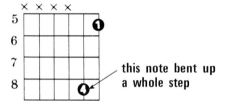

this note bent up a whole step

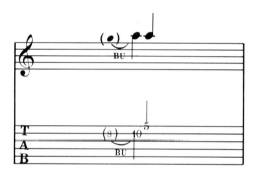

All octave double bends on the first and second strings may be played in this manner, anywhere up and down the neck, depending on what pitch is desired. Vibrato is almost always added by Hendrix.

Octave double bends are also played on the second and third strings. They are a little easier to play here because the stronger third finger does the bending. In our example the first finger plays the E on the second string, fifth fret. The third finger presses down the D on the third string, seventh fret, and bends this note up a whole step to E. It is the slight difference between the two E's that creates the edgy sound of this riff.

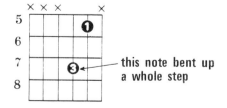

this note bent up a whole step

WITH ERIC BARRETT

I've written out the first measures of Jimi's solo in the masterful "Manic Depression." Notice that this song is in $\frac{3}{4}$ time, making it one of the strangest waltzes the world has ever heard. Jimi sets up the solo by playing the double-note octave bends as shown, and adds vibrato to the bent note. The solo is played over an A7 chord, outlined by the bass.

"Purple Haze"
© Copyright 1967 Six Continents
Music Publishing Inc., USA.
For the UK, British Commonwealth
(excluding Canada & Australasia) & Eire
Interworld Music Limited,
15 Berkely Street, London W1.
All rights reserved.
International copyright secured.

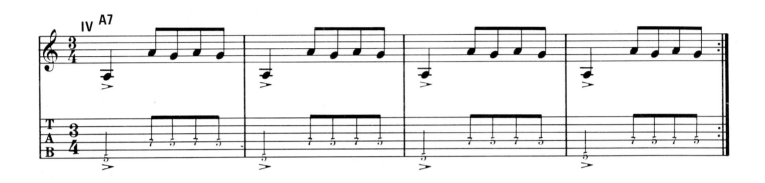

Over this riff, which is played by the bass an octave lower than written, Hendrix plays the following octave bands. Notice that they all have vibrato on the bent note. This takes a bit of practice but the effect is well worth it. The octave bends in the first and third measures take place on the second and third strings. The ones that begin in the fifth and seventh measures are played on the first and second strings. The Roman numerals tell you what position you are in. Hendrix doubles this part with his voice to further heighten its impact.

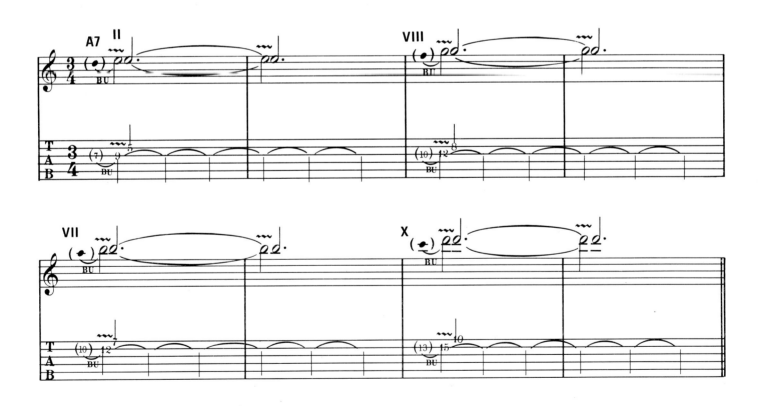

As a sort of summary of the Hendrix effects that we've talked about so far, I want to show you how to play the Introduction to "Purple Haze." This is the first song on the first side of Hendrix's first major release, so for many

AT ALBERT HALL, LONDON/ERIC HAYES

Purple Haze (intro)

Music by Jimi Hendrix

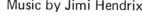

LINDA EASTMAN

people (myself included) it was the first exposure to Jimi's playing. For this reason, and because it's so striking and just plain rude, these measures of music have almost come to represent everything Jimi Hendrix stood for. Although this is not entirely fair, especially in light of his later development, "Purple Haze" is a beautiful piece that captures all the drugged, raging, sweet confusion that ushered in the psychedelic era.

The very first thing that you hear is the guitar playing octave B♭'s while the bass is hammering out quarter-note E's. (The song is mostly in E; E7 (#9) is the main chord.) This sets up a perfect, jarring dissonance that precedes the opening riff. But what really makes the intro so striking is the use of low open strings in the fourth and sixth measures. (The third and fourth measures are repeated note for note in the fifth and sixth measures.) Hendrix again utilizes open strings in the eighth measure.

The fifth measure contains a half-step bend that takes place on the fourth string; this is repeated two measures later. Pay attention to the effects; they are absolutely essential to the spirit of the music. Play it with a distortion effect on your guitar or (if you really want to get Jimi's sound) with a Marshall stack—all controls flat out—and a Stratocaster guitar. 'Scuse me while I kiss the sky!

Low-Note Riffs

Hendrix the guitarist is hard to separate from Hendrix the composer. When you listen to a Hendrix song, you are amazed at how full it sounds, as though a whole orchestra were condensed into a single Stratocaster guitar. That's the way he played, as those who were able to see him perform in person can attest.

It seems obvious that Jimi composed his songs on his guitar and worked out most of the parts that way. A consistent feature of many of his compositions is the prominent bass part, often played in whole or part by Jimi's guitar and doubled by the bass player. (Sometimes Hendrix played bass on his own records.) These low-note riffs are often derived from the older R&B styles that were Hendrix's roots.

This next example is the intro and beginning verse to "Fire."

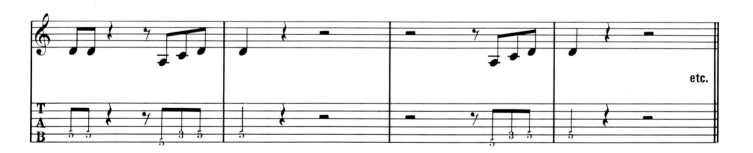

Here's the theme riff from the eerie "I Don't Live Today."

In "In from the Storm," from the *Cry of Love* album, Jimi plays a riff something like this to give this piece its rocking intensity.

BARRY PLUMMER

These riffs often take the place of straight chords, because they usually outline a chord; for instance, the above riff indicates F7. In "Who Knows," from the *Band of Gypsies* album (which is a live performance at the old Fillmore East), the band plays something like this next riff, outlining a C♯ to F♯ progression.

Hendrix combines a bass line with a small-note voicing in this opening riff to "Freedom" (*Cry of Love*).

In "Manic Depression" Hendrix uses low-note riffs to define most of the song. I've written out Jimi's part right up to the solo section. (See the section on double-note bends.) As we noted before, this song is in $\frac{3}{4}$ time, usually reserved for waltzes and ballads, but Hendrix's absolutely searing guitar makes this song burn from beginning to end.

"Manic Depression"
© Copyright 1967 Six Continents
Music Publishing Inc., USA.
For the UK, British Commonwealth
(excluding Canada & Australasia) & Eire
Interworld Music Limited,
15 Berkely Street, London W1.
All rights reserved.
International copyright secured.

46

Manic Depression

Music by Jimi Hendrix

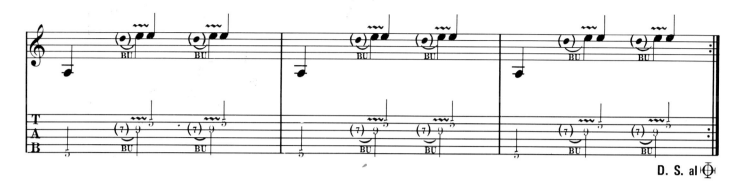

D. S. al ⊕

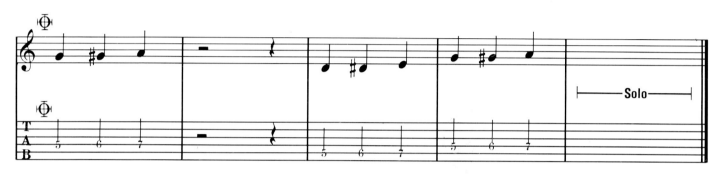

"Up From The Skies"

©Copyright 1967 Six Continents
Music Publishing Inc., USA.
For the UK, British Commonwealth
(excluding Canada & Australasia) & Eire
Interworld Music Limited,
15 Berkely Street, London W1.
All rights reserved.
International copyright secured.

BARRIE WEN-ZELL

Hendrix and the Blues

One of the most remarkable things about Jimi Hendrix was the fact that he pioneered modern rock guitar sounds in the most revolutionary way possible while still remaining firmly rooted in a blues tradition. There's blues in everything he plays, no matter what other effects are being utilized.

"Up from the Skies," for example, is one of Hendrix's most innovative songs. You hear jazz brushes from drummer Mitch Mitchell and some amazing talking wah-wah from Jimi. Listen closely and you'll hear some great Hendrix blues lines in his short but effective solo section. Try playing this with a wah-wah pedal to approximate Jimi's sound. The bend down with vibrato in the eighth measure is especially beautiful; and check out the extensive use of hammer-ons and pull-offs. These effects come straight from the blues. Also notice how Jimi uses the first phrase as a kind of theme or motif throughout the rest of the solo. Listen to the record!

Up From the Skies (solo)

Music by Jimi Hendrix

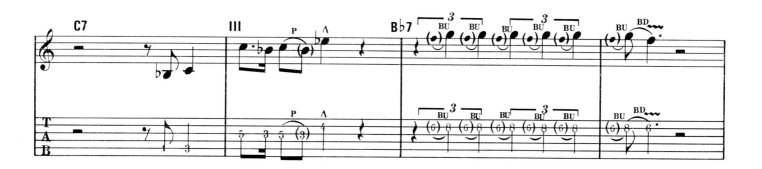

Listen to "Crosstown Traffic" for another example of a short, bluesy solo from Hendrix. It comes right after the lines, "All you do is slow me down, I got better things on the other side of town." At this point the chords modulate from a C7-F7 pattern to a G7 chord over which Jimi plays (and sings) a solo something like the following.

Hendrix's most striking blues performance on record has got to be "Voodoo Child," an extended jam on *Electric Ladyland*, featuring Stevie Winwood and Jack Cassidy supplementing the Experience. Besides taking some incredible solos, Jimi does some great filling behind his own singing that's right out of the blues tradition. During the verse about the mountain lion you can hear him play something like this. (Hendrix tunes his low E string down to D for this one.)

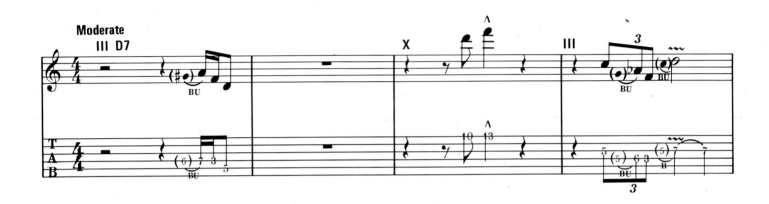

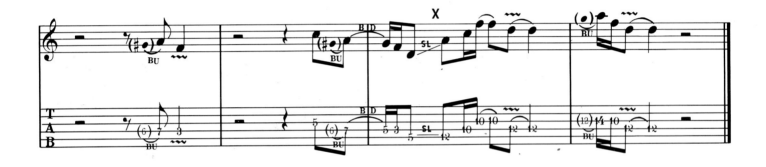

In the intro to "Freedom," Jimi's playing seems like a tribute to bluesmen such as Albert King and B.B. King. This makes sense in light of the Black consciousness content of the lyric and the social turmoil in American ghettos during this period. (Check out the liner photos on *Cry of Love.* "Freedom" is the first cut.) Anyway, Hendrix gives us some great blues playing here. Notice the long bend down in the second measure.

A slide up occurs in the third measure and a slide down in the fifth. I don't want you to get scared off because of the *leger lines* (little lines on which notes above or below the staff are written) so I've diagrammed the fingering below.

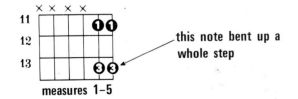

this note bent up a
whole step

measures 1–5

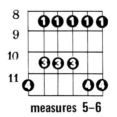

measures 5–6

"Freedom"
© Copyright 1968 World Song
Publishing Inc., USA.
For the YK, British Commonwealth
(excluding Canada & Australasia) & Eire
Interworld Music Limited,
15 Berkely Street, London W1.
All rights reserved.
International copyright secured.

Freedom (intro)

Music by Jimi Hendrix

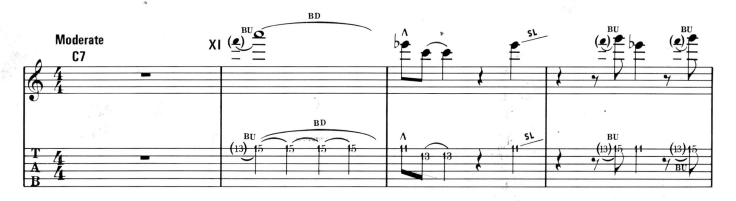

"Little Wing"— A Hendrix Classic

Besides being one of Hendrix's best lyrics, "Little Wing" (*Axis: Bold as Love*) stands as one of his most beautiful musical efforts as well. Musicians speak in awe of the song's wonderful chord structure and the way that Jimi brings it alive with his special way of playing chords.

I believe that Jimi had his guitar tuned down a half step when he recorded "Little Wing." For this reason, I've written it out in the key of E minor, instead of in E♭ minor where the actual sound of the notes lie. In this way, the open-string notes (especially the low sixth string, E) which are heard in the recording may be utilized as you work out the tune. If you're going to play with the record, I'd advise tuning your guitar to the recording as though it were in E minor. The following progression is the basis of the tune.

Well, she's walking through the clouds,
With a circus mind that's running wild,
Butterflies and zebras,
And moonbeams and fairy tales.
That's all she ever thinks about
Running with the wind.

When I'm sad, she comes to me,
With a thousand smiles she gives to me free.
It's alright, she says it's all right,
Take anything you want from me,
Anything.
Fly on, Little Wing.

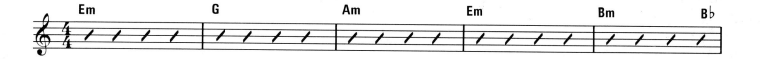

The first chorus of the song is played as an introduction by Jimi, unaccompanied except for some bell-chimes. In this intro almost all of the material that will be played during the vocal choruses is set out. There is some great chord work here, and you might want to review the chapter on Hendrix chords because Jimi uses all his favorite ballad devices. I've charted this intro out measure by measure because of the large number of hammer-ons and pull-offs, but as you get into it you'll notice how consistent Jimi's style is, and you'll start to pick up on what he's doing. Of course, working along with the recording is a tremendous help.

Check out the use of open strings, especially in the F to G measures (7, 16, and 26). Also, you'll really benefit as a guitarist if you carefully compare what Jimi plays with the chord symbol that he is working from. As for that massive slide that begins and ends his solo at the end of the tune, well, if you can figure out how he does it, please let me know. There are many effects that only Jimi knows how to play!

The solo itself is one of Jimi's most effective. Not that many notes are used, I've diagrammed the position you can use. The bends are the main item here. Again, notice how Jimi's note choice within a typical blues pattern works with the chords.

With the record, two notation systems, and the diagrams that follow the music you should be able to work this great piece out. After the first chorus, some sort of phasing has been added to Jimi's guitar, so if you have a phase-shifter you might want to use it.

"Little Wing"
© Copyright 1967 Six Continents
Music Publishing Inc., USA.
For the UK, British Commonwealth
(excluding Canada & Australasia) & Eire
Interworld Music Limited,
15 Berkely Street, London W1.
All rights reserved.
International copyright secured.

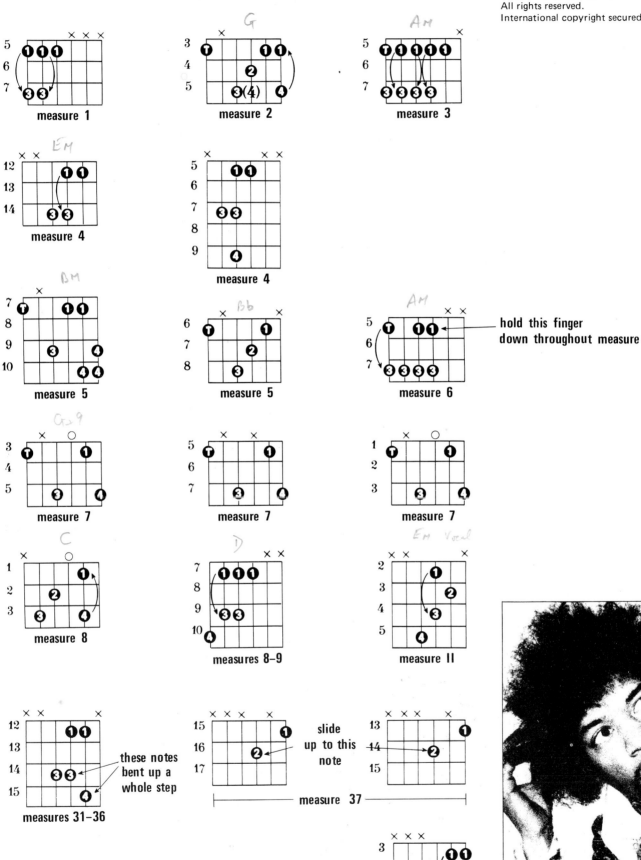

hold this finger
down throughout measure

these notes
bent up a
whole step

slide
up to this
note

H. GOODWIN

56

Little Wing

Music by Jimi Hendrix

The Recordings of Jimi Hendrix

Basically, the most valuable albums for studying Hendrix's guitar style are *Are You Experienced, Axis: Bold as Love,* and *Electric Ladyland.* These three represent the sounds that are most associated with Jimi Hendrix. Many of the others are of extreme interest, especially *Cry of Love,* which points out some new directions Hendrix was exploring before his death.

Alan Douglas has produced some albums (notably *Crash Landing*) that consist of tracks Jimi laid down during countless hours of experimenting in the studio with various other musicians backing him up. After Jimi's death, Douglas wiped out the tracks of the backup players and added new tracks with studio musicians of Douglas' own choosing.

Hendrix's live performances are featured on the following albums: *Electric Ladyland, Band of Gypsies, Live at Monterey, Woodstock* and *Woodstock Two* (Jimi with the Sky Church group).

LINDA EASTMAN

Below I've listed the songs and albums referred to in the text.

From *Are You Experienced*:
"Foxey Lady"
"Purple Haze"
"Love or Confusion"
"The Wind Cries Mary"
"Third Stone from the Sun"
"Fire"
"Manic Depression"
"I Don't Live Today"

From *Axis: Bold as Love*:
"Castles Made of Sand"
"Little Wing"
"All Along the Watchtower"
"Ain't No Telling"
"Up from the Skies"

From *Electric Ladyland*:
"Still Raining, Still Dreaming"
"Voodoo Child"
"Voodoo Child (slight return)"
"Crosstown Traffic"

From *Cry of Love*:
"Night Bird Flying"
"In from the Storm"
"Freedom"

From *Band of Gypsies*:
"Who Knows"

The following guide to Hendrix's recordings was compiled by Dr. Oldie.

I. Legitimate Jimi Hendrix Releases

	Title	Label	Date entered *Billboard* chart	Highest position
Singles	"Hey Joe"/ "51st Anniversary"	Reprise 0572	1967	did not chart
	"Purple Haze"/ "The Wind Cries Mary"	Reprise 0597	8/26/67	#65
	"Foxey Lady"/"Hey Joe"	Reprise 0641	12/23/67	#67
	"Up from the Skies"/ "One Rainy Wish"	Reprise 0665	3/16/68	#82
	"Foxey Lady"/"Purple Haze"	Reprise 0728	1968	did not chart
	"All Along the Watchtower"/ "Burning of the Midnight Lamp"	Reprise 0767	9/21/68	#20
	"Crosstown Traffic"/ "Gypsy Eyes"	Reprise 0792	11/30/68	#52
	"Stone Free"/"If Six Was Nine"	Reprise 0853	1969	did not chart
	"Freedom"	Reprise 1000	4/3/71	#59
	"Dolly Dagger"	Reprise 1044	10/23/71	#74

(After this point, no Hendrix singles made the charts.)

Albums				
	Are You Experienced	Reprise 6261	8/26/67	#5
	Axis: Bold as Love	Reprise 6281	2/10/68	#3
	Electric Ladyland	Reprise 6307	10/19/68	#1
	Smash Hits	Reprise 2025	8/2/69	#6
	Band of Gypsies (with Buddy Miles and Billy Cox)	Capitol 472	5/2/70	#5
	Live at Monterey	Reprise 2029	9/19/70	#16
	Cry of Love	Reprise 2034	3/6/71	#3
	Rainbow Bridge	Reprise 2040	10/9/71	#15
	Hendrix in the West	Reprise 2049	3/4/72	#12
	War Heroes	Reprise 2103	12/9/72	#48
	Jimi Hendrix	Reprise 6481	7/14/73	#89
	Crash Landing	Reprise 2204	3/22/75	#5
	Midnight Lightning	Reprise 2229	11/29/75	#43
	The Essential Jimi Hendrix	Reprise 2245	1978	did not chart

II. Cash-in Jimi Hendrix Releases (Generally speaking, what we have here are recordings Hendrix made as a side man with various groups. When Hendrix broke through, and again when he died, record companies dragged this stuff out and slapped Jimi's name on it.)

Single				
	"No Such Animal, Part I"/ "No Such Animal, Part 2" (with Curtis Knight)	Audio Fidelity 167	1967	did not chart

Albums				
	Get That Feeling (with Curtis Knight)	Capitol 2856	12/30/67	#75
	Flashing (with Curtis Knight)	Capitol 2894	1968	did not chart
	Get That Feeling & Flashing (with Curtis Knight)	Capitol 659		
	Two Great Experiences/ Together (with Lonnie Youngblood)	Maple 6004	3/20/71	#127
	In the Beginning (with the Isley Brothers)	T-Neck 3007		
	Rare Hendrix	Trip 9500	9/2/72	#82
	Roots of Hendrix	Trip 9501		
	Genius of Jimi Hendrix	Trip 9523		
	Superpak	Trip 3505		
	16 Greatest Hits	Trip 1622	1976	
	World of Jimi Hendrix	United Artists 505		

III. Oddities (Hendrix played on the following releases which are well-known in their own right.)

"Testify, Part 1"/ "Testify, Part 2" (the Isley Brothers)	T-Neck 501	1964	
"I Don't Know What You've Got But It's Got Me, Part 1"/"I Don't Know What You've Got But It's Got Me, Part 2" (Little Richard)	Vee Jay 698	11/27/65	#92

BARFIE WENTZELL